Living or Working with a

Bitch

Or

One of Her

Sons

A Stress Survival Guide

By

Richard Lindstrom, PhD.

A Note to the Reader

We believe reading this book will afford you the opportunity to evaluate your behavior and the behavior of those people with whom you associate. We have written the book in an easily understandable way. This book is not a presentation of Psychological Theory nor is it a presentation of Behavioral Therapy. It is however sound advice for many who hate or verbally mistreat others. We hope after reading this book many of you will improve your relationships. We also hope some people will adjust their behavior to be less apt to label people as a Bitch or a SOB. The book is not intended to be used as a tool to hurt but to help you. We would like to encourage politicians and the media to read the book twice and perhaps keep it as a reference companion whenever they feel tempted to attack or make hateful comments. We hope you have fun reading the book and perhaps gain a bit of insight into human behavior.

Dedication

The world can be a difficult place with wars, terror attacks, political disputes, fake news, corruption, natural disasters, and sometimes family crises. Adding living or working with a Bitch or S.O.B. can be a daunting task in life.

This book is in part dedicated to the many people in the world dealing with life who work hard, struggling to be happy and get along with unkind, difficult, selfish and often hurtful people in their family, work, or social lives.

But most of all it is dedicated to my strong and loving parents who lived their lives in love even through WWII and many other social, economic, and politically difficult times. They set a wonderful example to their six sons and countless others of how to treat family, friends, and one another with patience, understanding, tolerance, and most of all kindness.

Contents

Preface

Since you picked up this book you are at the very least curious about the subject. Is it just curiosity? Is it for fun? Or perhaps it is more serious? Is there a Bitch or a Son-of-a-Bitch in your life? Could someone you know be causing your blood pressure to rise when you are around them? Is there an extremely difficult person in your life who you believe is a Bitch or S.O.B.? Would you like to find out what you can do to help yourself or others determine if someone you know is really a Bitch or S.O.B.? Do you want the Bitch in your life to know what you and others think about their behavior? Maybe you want to help a Bitch or S.O.B. reform their lives and recover from their dysfunctional behavior? Do you want to tell the Bitch or S.O.B. off but feel you must find an anonymous way to do it for fear of the Bitch's reprisal? Maybe you want to find out if you, yourself, are a Bitch or S.O.B., and to what degree?

If some of these issues relate to your life, you probably won't be surprised to know you are not alone. Not by a long shot. Most of us have had to deal with a Bitch or S.O.B. at some point in our lives. Many of us face this problem far too often, and some of us deal face to face with them on a daily basis. The truth is, there is help for all of us who must deal with a Bitch or S.O.B. every single day of our lives.

I wrote this book because of the alarming growth in the number of Bitches and Sons-of-a-Bitches in America. It is estimated there are over fifteen million Bitches and S.O.B.s in the U.S. today wreaking havoc on the rest of us. We want these people stopped!

This book is intended to expose Bitch and S.O.B. tactics and strategies. We don't beat around the bush in revealing their self-serving, monstrous behavior. This book deals with Bitches and Sons-of-a-Bitches behavior in like manner. We do this because we believe many of their bad behaviors are quite similar, if not identical. Where there are differences, and there are, we outline them for you so you can be forewarned and forearmed.

Both the Bitch and her Sons are not just having a bad day or being moody, they are mean, rotten people the majority of the time. When they are civil, it is often only because they want something from someone or want to get even with someone. The Bitch and her Sons will find little comfort in this book unless they wish to reform. If you are the victim of a Bitch or S.O.B., here you will find the help you have been seeking. If your spouse or co-worker is getting to be Bitchier, you will be happy you discovered this book. It may save your marriage, your job, and even your life.

In this book, you will discover:

1. The definition of a "Bitch" and "Son-of-a-Bitch"

2. Profiles of their behavior
3. Explanations of their tactics
4. How to analyze your situation
5. How to measure the degree of your problem
6. How to increase your success in stopping a Bitch or S.O.B.
7. The tools required to put the Bitch or S.O.B in his or her place

You should know Bitches and Sons-of-Bitches are in every profession and in every part of the country. What's even more frightening is Bitches and S.O.B.s are in far too many homes. You may have thought Chicago, Los Angeles, and New York City had the majority of Bitches. This may be somewhat true, but Bitches have infiltrated every city, town, and facet of American life.

They are a plague which must be stopped. Like a virus, Bitch behavior tries to attack, contaminate, and destroy normal, healthy, and happy people. Like vampires, they suck the life blood from their victims whenever they have a chance. Well, we are here to help you stop them from hurting you, your family, relatives, friends, and co-workers.

We are sure you will benefit from what we tell you. This book may make you smile or laugh at how Bitches act. It may make you cry if the Bitch or S.O.B. is disrupting or destroying your life. This book is neither anti-men nor anti-women; it is anti-Bitch and anti-Son-of-a-Bitch. You will certainly find much truth in what we are sharing with you. If your life is perfect and yet untouched by a Bitch or S.O.B., you only need look around to see what they are doing to others. Are you next? It was a smart move to get this book now because "an ounce of prevention is worth a pound of cure." We want to emphasize every time the terms Bitch or S.O.B. are used in this book it refers to both the Bitch and her Sons.

Remember:

Men may be from Mars
Women may be from Venus
But one thing is for sure
Bitches and S.O.B.s are from
Hell.

Chapter Summaries

Chapters One and Two give the definitions of a Bitch and S.O.B. These chapters explain what a Bitch and S.O.B. are really like. It also covers the reasons we fear them. Believe us, you are not alone in your fear, there is no reason to be ashamed.

Chapter Three will help you survive with a Bitch in your home. You will find out just how much of a Bitch or S.O.B. is living with you. You will also learn their tactics and what you can do to protect yourself.

Chapter Four will cover the dangers of working with a Bitch or S.O.B. You won't want to miss this if you are suffering at work. Extensive Bitch research has uncovered invaluable data to aid you.

Chapter Five will show how Bitches and S.0.B.s are all around us. You can evaluate your list of famous people in politics, business, and entertainment. Judge for yourself who the Bitches and the S.0.B.s really are and compare their ratings.

Chapter Six tells us how Bitches and S.O.B.s become the way they are. In this section, you will learn the warning signs that exist. We also explain the psychological defenses we all must use to protect ourselves against the Bitch and her Sons and how to effectively utilize them.

Chapter Seven is key because it gives us the tools we need to combat the Bitch or the S.O.B. without risking our jobs or lives.

Chapter One

Are You a Bitch or a Son-of-a-Bitch?

We must first begin the book with a very important Question.

Do you feel self-conscious about being a Bitch or a Son-of-a-Bitch?

Do you feel the S.O.B. or Bitch inside you is trying to take control of your life? Do you find your behavior getting bitchier? Are others avoiding you? Are they telling you that you are always in a bad mood, mad, or upset? Let's take a brief self-assessment of your behavior now, so we can see where you are.

Circle One:	YES	NO	Sometimes
Does your behavior bother others?	Y	N	S
Do others worry about their relationship with you?	Y	N	S
Is your work suffering?	Y	N	S

Do others you live with want to move out?	Y	N	S
Do others you live with want you to move out?	Y	N	S
Do you embarrass your family?	Y	N	S
Do you dominate decisions?	Y	N	S
Do others hide from you in their own house or at work?	Y	N	S

If you answered "YES" to any of the above, you should read on.

Definition of a Bitch

According to Webster's Dictionary - A Bitch is: A lewd or immoral woman (or man, in the case of a Son-of-a-Bitch). A malicious, spiteful, and domineering woman (or man); an offensive person.

Let there be no mistake about it, we don't believe there is anything special or good about a Bitch or S.O.B. Whether men or women, these people are bad news to the rest of us.

A Bitch is an "itch" with a capitol "B" which stands for "bad."

B -- ad

I -- mpossible

T -- houghtless

C -- ontrolling

H -- ateful

The Bitch and her sons come in many shapes and sizes just like the rest of us. It is noteworthy at how this is one of those rare times that male and female behavior can be defined very much alike.

They (the Bitches and Sons of Bitches) behave the same way with few exceptions. Women can be very catty and may have more mood swings than her male counterparts but 80 percent of the time they behave in similar fashion with the same bad intentions toward other people. They are very unlike the rest of us.

There are many more Sons-of-Bitches than Bitches. The consensus is, and our research confirms, there are many more S.O.B.s due to breeding and social development. The fact that society has tolerated S.O.B.s more than Bitches adds to the greater number of S.O.B.s. The workplace is also a place where many S.O.B.s have developed over the years. Bitches are catching up though, because of the increase of women in the workforce and the decline of the moral structure in the U.S.

Although we fear Bitches close to us, you should know this author doesn't fear repercussions from Bitches and S.O.B.s who are offended by the writing of this book. As I see it, if Webster can define "Bitches," I can write about them and how they are poisoning our families, homes, workplaces, and lives.

If you think a Bitch is simply a woman who will not give a man his way, you are wrong (and you are probably a Son-of-a-Bitch, too). It is not a "feminist issue" either, although many do clearly qualify. Some women think any time a woman stands up for herself or for what she believes, men think she is a Bitch. WRONG! Many men are afraid of saying a woman is a Bitch for fear of other women thinking they are a chauvinistic Neanderthal. We do not subscribe to this Bitch phobia. If a behavior is bad, wrong, or immoral, we should be free to say so without being told we have a mysterious, underlying problem. Having a normal fear or disdain for immorality or meanness is healthy - not phobic. We do feel, however, the terms "Bitch" and "Son-of-a-Bitch" are used too often and incorrectly. People who simply do things we do not agree with but are honest in their actions with no intention to hurt anyone are not Bitches.

The female term "Bitch" is the official term for a female dog. It was initially used in a negative connotation for female dogs who behaved badly. It was later used for women who acted badly. Some women who constantly complained without justification were said to be "Bitchy" or "Bitching." Complaining men or women are now often called "Bitches and S.O.B.s". Both women and men have developed many derogatory terms for one another. Women seem to be more adept than men at developing these terms.

The following commonly used terms are used to describe Bitches and Sons of a Bitch.

Bitches	Sons of Bitches
Nag	Brute
Catty	Bastard
Slut	Scum
Witch	Wimp
Shrew	Dog
Dog	Pig
Hag	Monster
Gold Digger	Fag
Wench	Knuckle Dragger
Loose	Playboy
Whore	Animal
Tease	Mole
Tramp	Neanderthal
Butch	Louse
Bimbo	Chauvinist
Broad	Dope
Domineering	Jerk
Feminist	Loser
Women's Libber	Toad
Hysterical	Pimp
Spiteful	Coward
Bag	Hustler
Amazon	Worm
Virago	Snake
Vixen	Slime
Termagant	Sleaze
Battle Axe	Deadbeat
Frump	Bum
Fallen Woman	Slug
Dame	Failure

Arm Candy	Leach
Slag	Idiot
Fishwife	Sucker
Vamp	Barbarian
Scarlet	Bear
Slut	Rat
Minx	Grouch
Coquette	Cad
Floozy	Bitch
Goer	Pretender
Jezebel	Spiteful
Scrubber	Blackguard
Strumpet	Roughneck
Seductress	Tyrant
Nymph	Zealot
Zealot	Swine
Bully	Bully

***Please Note:** In the book, we point out a vast amount of negative terms for women which is far and away excessive. This unfair treatment of women is an area worthy of study but is not the subject for this book.*

It is also important to point out these terms are often used to respond to or describe women who stand up for themselves or speak their mind. This, too, is not addressed by this book.

It should be noted that we also recognize cases of use of the term "Bitch" as terms of affection or humor as in "My Bitch, A good Bitch, or Funny Bitch." We think it is neither funny nor affectionate.

The book attempts only to examine the use of the terms Bitch and S.O.B. when dealing with difficult people in difficult situations.

Now, we know some of you are still wondering if you are a Bitch or S.O.B. Some Bitches are wondering what will happen if more people lose their fear or phobia and begin calling them the Bitches they truly are. What will they do if they can no longer hide behind the feminine shield which has protected them? You know the one - who makes other men and women fearful of being labeled sexist or biased against women's equality because they don't think Bitch behavior has a place among civilized men and women?

If you must ask if you are a Bitch, then you probably spend at least some time being a Bitch. Maybe you are even afraid of being dominated by your inner Bitch forces. We can help, but now we would like to attempt to reveal Bitch behavior.

We want you to take a little quiz. You may evaluate someone you know as well as yourself. Of course, the real Bitch or S.O.B. will have a strong inclination not to take this quiz because they are very clear about who they are and do not want to change. God forbid anyone else discovers the Bitch failed one of our Bitch or S.O.B. quizzes. If you meet someone who has refused to take this test, chances are very good - they are a Bitch or S.O.B. If you want to quickly look at the behavior of someone you know and suspect of being a Bitch or one of her Sons - this is your first chance. There will be more later.

Check the personality traits which apply to you or someone you know.
Put the possible Bitch's or S.O.B.'s Name Here:

____

☐ Negative	☐ Obnoxious
☐ Aggressive	☐ Believes in their perfection
☐ Inflexible	☐ Mean
☐ Controlling	☐ Self-Righteous
☐ Know it all	☐ Arrogant
☐ Must have own way	☐ Possesses a huge ego
☐ Yells	☐ Emotionally abusive
☐ Grouchy	☐ Makes fun of people
☐ Hostile	☐ Often loud
☐ Doesn't "get it"	☐ Bully
☐ Suspicious/Paranoid	☐ Chronic Complainer
☐ Opinionated to a fault	☐ Spiteful
☐ Impatient	☐ Not compassionate
☐ Unkind	☐ Unfair or Unjust
☐ Not understanding	☐ Not a good person
☐ No conscience	☐ Causes everyone stress
☐ Wears "nice" face mask	☐ Possesses a strong sense of entitlement

☐ Hurtful or harassing

☐ Does not believe in fair play

☐ Not sympathetic (consequently, pathetic comes to mind)

☐ Believes in dictatorial leadership

☐ Not moral, lacks positive values

☐ If not lacking in manners altogether, then certainly lacking terribly in one area or another

Now add up all the check marks and put the total here ____________.

Scoring is based on the number of check marks:

Moody = 0-5
Bitchy = 6-10
Bitch or S.O.B. = 11-15
Super Bitch or S.O.B = 15+

Super Bitch or S.O.B. = 15+. You may never reform this Bitch or one of her many Sons. There is only a slight chance of recovery here. The recovery rate is so low because they honestly enjoy being Bitchy. It usually takes an act of God to change them. Even then, they often become domineering and controlling personalities. You can't win with these people! They live to terrorize.

Bitch or S.O.B. = 11-15. This Bitch or S.O.B. is usually found at work or when dealing with other people but are not necessarily a Bitch or a S.O.B. when alone or asleep. This person is often difficult to be around for more than a minute or two.

Bitchy = 6-10. These individuals have fleeting Bitch moments.

Moody = 0-5. This person can be an awful grump or nag, but only at times. You should take care to see that they don't progress. They are not yet possessed and at this stage will still listen to reason.

A Personal Evaluation

What you think of yourself is very important, certainly, but please do not discount what others think of you as well as what you think of others. Each is equally important.

Answer these questions about someone you know.

Name:_______________________________________

Circle the best response.

This person believes he/she:

	Almost Always	Often	Sometimes	Never
Is an angel or Saint.	0	0	5	10
Is an especially nice person.	0	5	10	15
Has his/her ups and downs.	15	10	5	0
Is moody.	15	10	5	0
Is kind of Bitchy.	15	10	5	0
Is Bitchy a lot.	15	10	5	0

Is a Bitch.	15	10	5	0
Is a Bitch and proud of it. He/She works hard at being a Bitch or a S.O.B and believes being nice is for suckers and wimps.	15	10	5	0

Total Points______________________

His/her friends view him/her as:

	Almost Always	Often	Sometimes	Never
An angel or saint.	0	0	5	10
An especially nice person.	0	5	10	15
Having his/her ups and downs.	15	10	5	0
Moody a lot.	15	10	5	0
Kind of Bitchy.	15	10	5	0
Bitchy a lot.	15	10	5	0
A full-fledged Bitch or S.O.B.	15	10	5	0

Total Points_________________________

His/her relatives view him/her as:

	Almost Always	Often	Sometimes	Never
An angel or saint.	0	0	5	10
An especially nice person.	0	5	10	15
Having his/her ups and downs.	15	10	5	0
Moody a lot.	15	10	5	0
Kind of Bitchy.	15	10	5	0
Bitchy a lot.	15	10	5	0
A full-fledged Bitch or S.O.B.	15	10	5	0

Total Points ________________________

His/her co-workers view him/her as:

	Almost Always	Often	Sometimes	Never
An angel or saint.	0	0	5	10
An especially nice person.	0	5	10	15
Having his/her ups and downs.	15	10	5	0
Moody a lot.	15	10	5	0
Kind of Bitchy.	15	10	5	0
Bitchy a lot.	15	10	5	0
A full-fledged Bitch or S.O.B.	15	10	5	0

Total Points _________________________

Other acquaintances view him/her as:

	Almost Always	Often	Sometimes	Never
An angel or saint.	0	0	5	10
An especially nice person.	0	5	10	15
Having his/her ups and downs.	15	10	5	0
Moody a lot.	15	10	5	0
Kind of Bitchy.	15	10	5	0
Bitchy a lot.	15	10	5	0
A full-fledged Bitch or S.O.B.	15	10	5	0

Total Points ________________________

Write the score in the space below for each group's point of view.

	0	10	20	30	40	50	60	70	80	90	100
Personal View											
Friend's View											
Relative's View											
Co-Worker's View											
Acquaintance's View											
	Angel	**Nice**		**Normal**		**Moody**		**Bitchy**		**Bitch**	

Remember, this is how you think others view the person. If you really want to know what they truly believe, ask a few of these people to fill out the questionnaire. Sometimes the truth hurts, but it almost always helps if the person desires help.

Various groups view people differently, but when the majority of people see a person as a Bitch, that point of view should not be discounted. You may even want to evaluate your own behavior more closely because you certainly don't want to accuse others if you are, in fact, more of a Bitch or S.O.B. than you think.

Chapter Two
Who's Afraid of the Big Bad Bitch?

Some may fear the Bitch who breathes but we should all fear the Bitch who breeds.

Fear of a Bitch or Son-of-a-Bitch is natural. Bitches and Sons-of-Bitches create enormous amounts of undue stress in every environment and with every person in whom they come into contact. They create what is called a "Red Zone" or "Danger Zone." Whether at work, at home, or in between, people in a Bitch's Red Zone cannot wait for the Bitch to leave.

When the Bitch leaves, people feel the environmental stress decrease, like air rushing out of an over-filled balloon. When the S.O.B. stops blowing stress in, people relax. When the Bitch blows harder and creates greater pressure, the tension and fear within the environment becomes unbearable.

Sometimes, the Bitch ties a knot in the balloon and tries to cut off the release of pressure. Anyone who knows the S.O.B. knows when they have entered the Bitch's Red Zone. If you are not concerned about a Bitch's Red Zone, you are either nuts, dumb, or naïve.

There are three zones.

- **Red or Danger** - The Bitch is in your immediate area.
- **Yellow or Caution** - The S.O.B. is in visual range.
- **Green or Safety** –You are safely out of range of the Bitch or S.O.B.

If you are in the "Red Zone" you should be in fear for your own safety. You should be on "Red Alert" with your guard up. Sometimes, there are a number of Bitches or S.O.B.s in the same area of different territories they frequent; therefore, they create various caution boundaries where

you may encounter them. This is true even though they generally tend to stay out of one another's territory.

The Bitch creates three kinds of stress in a **Red Zone**:

Bitch Stress

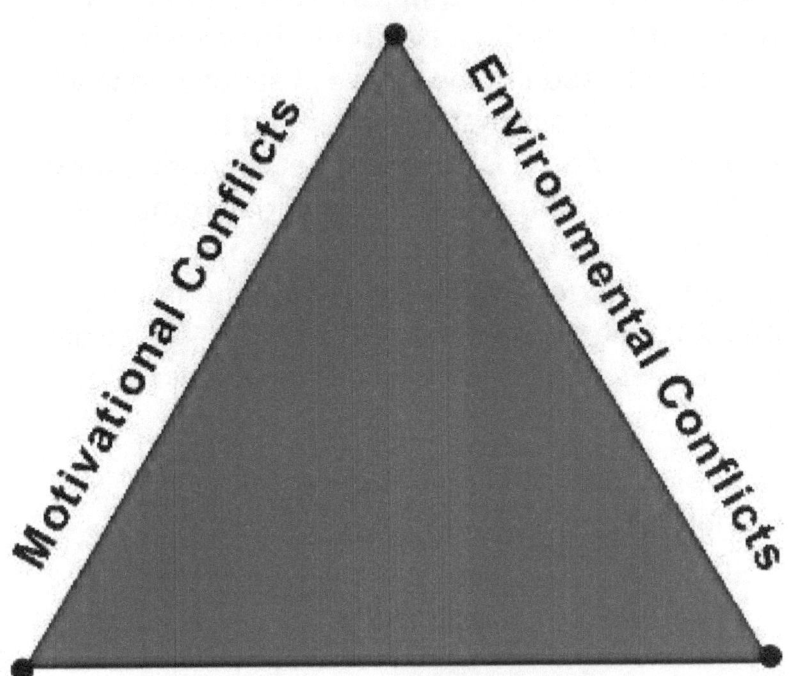

Environmental Stress is the frustration brought on by situations like Bitches in traffic, S.O.B.s making social policies, and Bitches controlling company procedures.

Personal Emotional Stress is the frustration due to a Bitch setting understated or unrealistic aspirations which affect others. Improvised performance, a lack of the Bitch's job knowledge or credentials, even the Bitch's lack of practice or ability puts stress on us. When the S.O.B. breaks promises in a relationship or on the job they can also cause a good deal of stress.

Motivational Stress is the frustration as a result of t h e S.O.B. having to make difficult choices. These choices have distinctly positive and negative alternatives affecting us. For example, when a Bitch must set a priority, they often procrastinate and use avoidance behavior, they vacillate, and sometimes even ignore the problem altogether. These actions negatively affect us all. Look at the chart below – illustrating how stress can build from a Bitch's actions or lack of actions.

Multiple Bitch or S.O.B. Levels of Stress Conflicts:

LOW	STRESS	HIGH
Environmental	Personal	Motivational

You can also see in the chart below how multiple levels of Bitch stress conflicts can also occur when environmental, personal, and motivational issues build on each other. When this happens, the Bitch stress can be overwhelming.

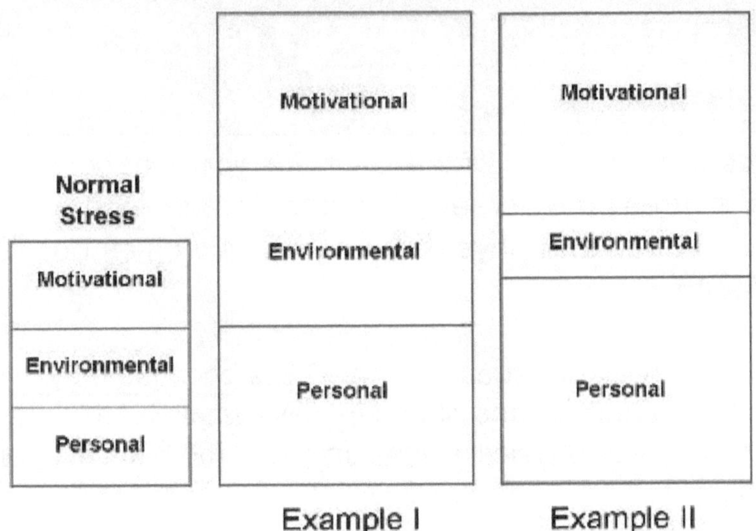

Notice Normal Stress is balanced and under control. Examples I and II show how a great deal of stress can build up in different ways, allowing the stress in our lives to get out of proportion in one or more areas.

We can deal with our stress in either positive or negative ways. The list below illustrates positive and negative ways of dealing with Bitch stress.

Positive or Enhanced Behavior	Negative or Hindered Behavior
Is Normal	Is Normal
Expression	Anger
Excitement	Disgust
Acceptance	Sadness
Satisfaction	Dissatisfaction

We are all fearful of the Bitch for good reasons. The stress they create threatens our personal, emotional, and physical integrity as well as our health.

We get negative stress from S.O.B.s because they project it onto us and others in ways which lead to emotional or physical illness. In short, the bitch makes us sick!

We all set goals in our lives. When these goals and aspirations become blocked by a Bitch at work or in our personal lives, the result is stress and frustration. We do not become emotional or stressed over issues unless we care about them or are motivated by them. How we deal with the stress from S.O.B.s depends on our coping resources and our knowledge of the consequences.

A healthy person deals with most disappointments by seeking the support of friends and relatives. They help us analyze situations, weighing the alternatives, and then selecting, trying, and re-trying changes in behavior. We may then set different, less stressful goals. We also may leave the Red Zone for a less threatening environment.

A Bitch often chooses the alternative for us. She chooses the option which satisfies her personal and always selfish goal. The rest of us, be damned.

**Physical Symptoms
The Emotional Components of Bitch or
S.O.B. Stress Affecting Others Includes:**

Pounding Heart
Tenseness
Dry Throat
Digestive Issues
Confusion
Grouchy Moods
Poor Sleep Habits
Resentfulness
Irritability
Trembling
Sweating
Poor Appetite
Memory Loss
Fatigue

Uncontrolled, abnormal S.O.B. stress responses result in our prolonged emotional upset. Living with Bitch stress and dealing with the tension and negative emotions of S.O.B.s can smother us. Positive behaviors come from handling Bitch stress with tools such as normal expression, understanding, sadness, and self-assessment. Hindered behavior comes from handling Bitch stress with anger, disgust, resentment, depression, or aggression.

The S.O.B. wants you to behave in a negative way. They know we dread acting badly and they take advantage of this fact. They do so to point it out to you as well as others. Shoving your mistakes in your face and embarrassing you is where they excel. The Bitch wants to step up and get ahead and you are the step they use to do so.   It also makes them feel justified in their behavior and thus superior to you. Do not give them the chance, but be careful not to overreact to their abnormal behavior. The following chart shows different reactions and how these reactions can get out of control.

People Respond Differently to Bitch or S.O.B. Stress in Their Lives

LOW STRESS   **HIGH STRESS**

Reactions

Normal	Emotional	Aggression	Physical
Excitement	Avoidance	Tantrums	Headaches
Happiness	Outbursts	Threats	Heart Disease
Satisfaction	Yelling	Vandalism	Injuries
	Crying	Assault	Cancer
	Dissatisfaction	Verbal Attacks	Depression
		Fighting	Illness
			Blood Pressure

How we react to the Bitch or S.O.B. can make a world of difference in regard to our sanity. Check the chart above. It shows various ways of dealing with Bitch and S.O.B. stress, including the good, the bad, and the ugly.

The Negative Effects of Prolonged Bitch or S.O.B. Stress Includes:

Emotional outbursts such as yelling, crying, depression, and avoidance. Aggression in the form of tantrums, verbal attacks, threats, vandalism, and criminal assault.

There are Multiple Bitch or S.O.B. Levels of Stress Conflicts:

Normally the progression of chronic stress will range from emotional upset to illness; but depending on the individual, it can also include an emotional progression to aggression before illness.

A single example cannot possibly illustrate all the reasons why we should fear a Bitch. It does boil down to this: The S.O.B. can and often does hurt others at home and at work. The most troublesome issue is being a Bitch or S.O.B. is LEGAL.

The Bitch's unreasonable and disrespectful behavior creates fear in us because, in its extreme, his or her bad conduct sets him or her apart from the normal person with exaggerations of behaviors found in every human being.

In short, we can all be moody, Bitchy, a Bitch, or

a Son-of-a- Bitch occasionally. It takes hard work, dedication, and a disdain for someone to be a Bitch all the time. A full-time Bitch will almost always be disagreeable, reacting badly to people, as well as life and its circumstances.

Do we fear the Bitch because we believe they are possessed by evil spirits? Are they mentally ill? Should we put them in a mental hygiene program? Can we have them committed to a mental health hospital or force them into therapy?

Sorry, but there are not any S.O.B. wards in existence, not yet anyway. It is not because there is no demand; it is simply that there is no formal classification of Bitch disorders. We all fear them, so should we imprison them? Should we sentence them to five years of being nice? Some Bitches would rather be put in prison than have to be nice to people.

Well, the truth is we cannot do any of these things, but we can protect ourselves.

Remember:

To the Bitch,

<u>MALE</u>

means

<u>M</u>en

<u>A</u>re

<u>L</u>ess

<u>E</u>qual.

Chapter Three
Living with a Bitch or a Son-of-a-Bitch

When you get in your car to drive home, do you begin to sweat, start to tremble, experience muscle spasms, and generally dread your arrival at home? If this is the case, there may be a Bitch just inside your door waiting to pounce on you with a rude, nagging, and relentlessly vicious verbal attack. Do you look for extra work to do to delay your arrival at home? Do you leave home for work earlier and earlier each morning? Does this person, your suspect, treat you with constant hostility and anger? Does it seem like as if he or she resents your very existence? If this is the case, you have Big Bitch or S.O.B. problems.

The consequences of living with a Bitch or a Son-of-a-Bitch, according to our national sampling of S.O.B. patterns at home, show a variety of forms which all possess a fairly simple pattern:

- The Bitch develops a twisted view of the world and thereby creates an unusually high threat of increased stress to those around them.
- The pattern features chronic dissatisfaction, even when there are large amounts of success or gratification in the Bitch's life. They generally

do not enjoy anything. They have an eternally unsatisfied need to control and criticize everything.

Review the list on the following page and determine if any detail applies to the Bitch or S.O.B. with whom you live.

Bitch and S.O.B. Alert

This list can help you recognize if you or someone you know is in a relationship with a S.O.B.

Simply check the blocks which apply to the person you name. The more blocks checked, the more dangerous the situation.

Name:_______________________________________

☐ **Nagging Criticism**: Name-calling, mocking, blaming, yelling, swearing, making humiliating remarks or gestures
☐ **Pushy**: Rushing you to make decisions
☐ **Manipulating**: Others against you
☐ **Bossy**: Always claiming to be right, constantly telling you what to do in a demanding way
☐ **Disrespect**: Interrupting, changing topics, not listening or responding, twisting your words, putting you down in front of others, insulting your friends or family
☐ **Untrustworthy**: Lying, withholding information, cheating on you, being overly jealous, stealing your ideas, following you as if you are under investigation
☐ **Emotional Withholding**: Not expressing feelings; not giving support, attention, or compliments; not respecting your feelings, rights, or opinions
☐ **Dominating**: Preventing or making it difficult for you to work with others or visit friends or relatives,

monitoring your phone calls, telling you where you
can and cannot go
- **Harassment:** Checking up on you, embarrassing
  you in public, refusing to leave when asked,
  following you from room to room, taunting and
  antagonizing you into fights or arguments
- **Controlling**: Manipulating or scheming the
  outcome or certain circumstances and situations to
  benefit themselves

Take This Bitch Quiz

Answer the questions about each person you live with who you suspect may be a Bitch or a Son-of-a-Bitch.

Question	Always	Often	Some-times	Never
Does the person devalue your opinion?	4	3	2	1
Does the person dominate conversations?	4	3	2	1
Does the person feel you are a failure, a bum, a slug, a wimp, or inadequate?	4	3	2	1
Does the person try to control most household decisions?	4	3	2	1
Is the person rude?	4	3	2	1
Is the person overbeari	4	3	2	1
Does the person smoke or drink too much?	4	3	2	1
Does the person take drugs?	4	3	2	1

Question	Always	Often	Some-times	Never
Is the person super-critical?	4	3	2	1
Is the person egotistical?	4	3	2	1
Is the person overly stubborn?	4	3	2	1
Is the person a troublemaker?	4	3	2	1
Is the person ungrateful?	4	3	2	1
Is the person insensitive to others?	4	3	2	1
Is the person self-important?	4	3	2	1
Is the person harsh?	4	3	2	1
Does the person get hysterical?	4.	3	2	1
Does the person nit-pick?	4	3	2	1
Does the person nag?	4	3	2	1
Is the person impolite?	4	3	2	1
Is the person selfish?	4	3	2	1

Question	Always	Often	Some-times	Never
Is the person self-centered?	**4**	**3**	**2**	**1**
Is the person mean?	4	3	2	1
Is the person bossy?	4	3	2	1
Is the person conceited?	4	3	2	1
Is the person thoughtless?	4	3	2	1
Is the person over-reactive?	4	3	2	1
Is the person unreasonable?	4	3	2	1
TOTAL	____	____	____	____

Score 4 points for each "Always" answer.
Score 3 points for each "Often" answer.

Score 2 points for each "Sometimes" answer.
Score 1 point for each "Never" answer.

Angel/Saint = 0 - 10 Points

This is a wonderful person. Marry this person. If they want something, get it or do it for them.

Special = 11 - 25 Points

This is a good person. You should feel proud to be related to or associated with them. Do what you can to develop an even stronger relationship.

Nice = 26 - 35 Points

This person goes out of their way to do good deeds but sometimes makes mistakes.

Normal = 36 - 49 Points

This is a good person with human flaws which should be tolerated or overlooked from time to time. Stick with them.

Difficult/Moody = 50 - 60 Points

This person gets upset or mad a bit too often. You should be careful they do not have a negative effect on your family. Try to talk things over more often. These people can be biased, untrustworthy, and sometimes self-serving.

Bitchy/Bad = 61 - 70 Points

This person is living on the edge. Protect yourself from undue stress and heartache. You need to seriously evaluate your relationship to prevent disaster. Protect any children from exposure to this person's negative behavior. They can be sneaky, deceiving, vindictive, and unreasonable.

Bitch or S.O.B. = 71 - 89 Points

This person is a Bitch. You need to create a plan for self-defense before it is too late. You have only one life; why live it with a S.O.B.?

Super Bitch or S.O.B. = 90 - 112 Points

This person is a reign of terror; miserable plus miserable for anyone within range. Seek "E.B.T." (Emergency Bitch Treatment). Consider moving as soon as possible.

If You Are Living with A Bitch or A S.O.B.,

You Are Not Alone.

It is estimated there are three million full-fledged Bitches and eight million Sons-of-Bitches living in the U.S. alone, about three percent of the population. In 2000, the estimates were 500,000 Bitches and two million Sons-of-Bitches. This demonstrates a dramatic increase in both groups, but the increase in Bitches is alarming. As pointed out in Chapter Two, the reasons for the increase is the breakdown of U.S. morals especially as seen on T.V. The breakdown of the U.S. family structure, including the increase in divorce, crime, abortion, and pornography have all added to the problem.

More frightening is the increase in Bitchy people. These people often will not stop until they get their way and make everyone else miserable. They may start a relationship with what appears to be love and devotion, then move in to seize economic control, abusing any authority available to them.

Both the Bitch and the Son-of-a-Bitch seek out wimps and drain everything they can from these relationships. Here is the Bitch's and the S.O.B.'s view of a _wimp:_

Bitch's View   **Son-of-a-Bitch's View**

The

Woman

Is

Most

Powerful

The

Wimp

Is

My

Property

Bitch or S.O.B. Trap

Guide to the Relationship Stages of the Bitch or S.O.B.

Watch out! You could be trapped before you know it. This guide explains how the Bitch or S.O.B. trap works. Once the relationship begins, there are ten stages – each listed here.

1. **Nice person** (So you think.)

2. **I love you** (The lie.)

3. **Seduction** (The trap is set.)

4. **Commitment/Marriage** (The trap is sprung.)

5. **Concern** (You first realize you have a problem.)

6. **Tension** (You first see them for what they are and try to resist.)

7. **Intimidation** (They squash your resistance; the abuse begins.)

8. **Control** (They know you love them, and they take advantage. They are a full-time Bitch or S.O.B. now.)

9. **Power** (They try to dominate.)

10. **Victory (**They try to dictate everything. You must seek help to survive.)

The timing of these stages differs from Bitch to Bitch and S.O.B. to S.O.B. depending on the strength of his or her victim. If you are too strong for the Bitch to control fully, they may cease to acknowledge your existence and become a roadblock preventing you from moving on with your life without them. If you live and also work with the S.O.B., you are in big trouble. Keep reading.

Chapter Four
Working with a Bitch or a Son-of-a-Bitch

One of the most dangerous things you can do is work for/with a Bitch or a Son-of-a-Bitch

Imagine this – it is morning. You and millions of Americans awake and reality sets in. Your dream of hitting the lottery is over. It's now time to go to work and face the S.O.B. you daily dread. Quickly your anxiety rises as you approach the door at work. When you enter the building, you feel the tension growing. As most employees grab their morning coffee, you, instead, reach deep into your pocket, desperately, searching for your antacid. A double dose is the minimum needed to begin your workday. As the day goes on you will consume at least a dozen tablets and half a bottle of the pink stuff.

By 11:00 A.M., you fantasize about not seeing the S.O.B. today. All of a sudden, the S.O.B. calls your name and your heart sinks. The chill ravages your body like fingernails scraping across a chalkboard. As you move toward his domineering pose, a co-worker passes, and without moving his head for fear the S.O.B. will see, gives you a pitiful look as he whispers, "good luck." With a deep breath, you reply silently, "thanks." You continue on your way, knowing your fate will include relentless verbal abuse from which there is no escape.

This is a taste of what it is like for the millions who have to work for a S.O.B. or Bitch. You probably know this scenario all too well.

Can you believe this is how many people start and end their workday? What an awful way to feel! These S.0.B.s cause a tremendous amount of stress because of how they treat others. Most of us can envision the S.0.B.s résumé listing the Nazi SS as their previous employer. Maybe we also imagine a Bitch's job assessment reading a little like the following:

Bitch's Name_______________________________________

Title____

Department____

Leadership: This person is exceptional at placing fear into the hearts of all employees with whom they come in contact.

Judgment: They prejudge employees without exception. They never weigh the impact of their actions on the work or morale of other employees.

Problem Analysis: They have no ability to define problems. They use exceptional finger pointing and blaming techniques to the exclusion of sound logical fact finding.

Planning/Organizing: They cannot arrange work systematically nor can they set priorities or establish an appropriate course of action. They never make wise use of resources - especially their colleagues, co-workers, and subordinates.

Communications: They effectively rant, rave, scream, and threaten others whenever possible. They have no persuasive skills. They are always intentionally vague and unclear in their interactions with others.

Work Relations: They are unstable in their performance when under the slightest pressure. They cannot be counted on to be fair, honest, or carry out their responsibilities.

Career Goals: They try to get ahead at the expense of others. They are committed to making others look bad in order to have as little competition as possible. They suck up to supervisors whenever and wherever possible.

Productivity: They have a negative effect on the workplace which results in absenteeism. They negatively affect the productivity of others.

The Effect on People in Organizations

We did research on Bitch and S.O.B. stress in the workplace. We found employers and employees alike, felt strongly about the stress caused by Bitchy behavior in the workplace. Bitches and Sons-of-Bitches are responsible for billions of dollars of lost productivity and increased health care cost annually.

National Poll of the Top Ten Areas of Stress Related Absenteeism

1. The Boss is a Son-of-a-Bitch.

2. I work for/with a Bitch.

3. Drug Addiction

4. Alcoholism

5. Depression

6. Marital

7. Family

8. Kids

9. Medical

10. Other Stress Related

From the Employee's Perspective

Our research shows 92 percent of all Americans agree that personal psychosocial stress problems spill over into work resulting in decreased productivity. It is frightening, but more than 40 percent of American workers say they have experienced stress-related problems from a Bitch or S.O.B. at work. Thirty percent of workers say Bitches and Sons-of-a-Bitches are major distractions at work. The employees who stated they believe stress training support programs can help with personal and work problems was an overwhelming 63 percent.

From the Employer's View

From the research, we found a majority of employers agreed attendance (46 percent), productivity (43 percent), and emotional well- being (41 percent) are harmfully affected by employees personal and workplace stress caused by Bitches or S.O.B.s. Personal problems are considered detrimental to productivity from Bitches and S.O.B.s. Employers also are clear that employees with Bitchy behavior are a major deterrent to productivity. Employers say 26 percent of their employees have mood swings ranging from mild (25 percent) to severely Bitchy (five percent).

Unscheduled absenteeism hovers around three percent accounting for 550 million days lost annually in the U.S. alone representing a cost of $300 billion to the national economy. We think Bitches and S.O.B.s are one of the major reasons employee absenteeism. Employees average three days out of work for every 100 days. Firms employing 100 to 250 people suffered a 22 percent jump in unscheduled absences, while larger corporations of 5,000 and over lost $1.6 million to absenteeism.

Workers who are driven to drink and skip work in order to avoid Bitch or S.O.B. psychosocial stress related problems are also being created by Bitches and S.O.B.s. They account for 47 percent of the absences from work each year. Other areas related to absenteeism included personal illness, family issues, and personal needs. Bitch stress accounts for 25 percent of employee terminations and 20 percent of industrial accidents.

You can see from the statistics Bitch and S.O.B. stress is having a devastating impact on the workplace.

Psychosocial training pays off for companies with a Bitch or S.O.B. problem. Research findings from a nationwide survey of U.S. companies showed company costs due to S.O.B. stress related workplace problems can be reduced through stress training and support.

Companies have saved as much as 300 percent on every dollar invested in employee training and assistance programs to reduce stress related problems in the workplace.

Most Frequent Stress Related Problems Affecting Productivity

1.   Substance Abuse

2.   Mental Health

3.   Family/Marital

4.   Job Stress from a Bitch or S.O.B.

5.   Working Conditions

6.   Supervisory Training

7.   Organization Downsizing

8.   Security Concerns

9.   Wellness and Health

10.   Organizational Restructuring

11.   Benefits Communication

12.	Occupational Health

The more acute and chronic the stress employees have from the Bitch, the greater the chance of this stress hurting their work and personal lives. This is clearly pointed out in the next chart.

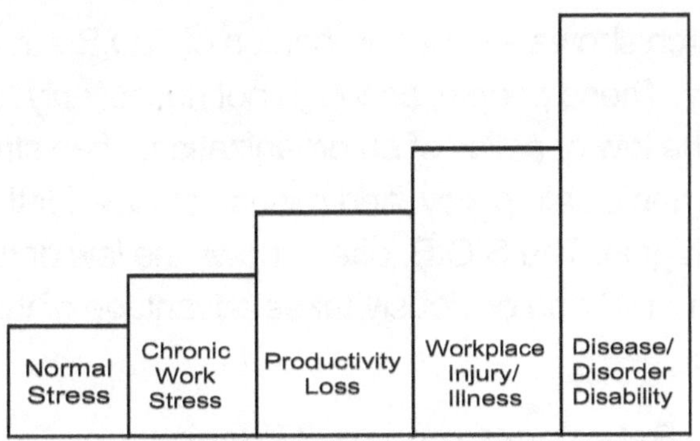

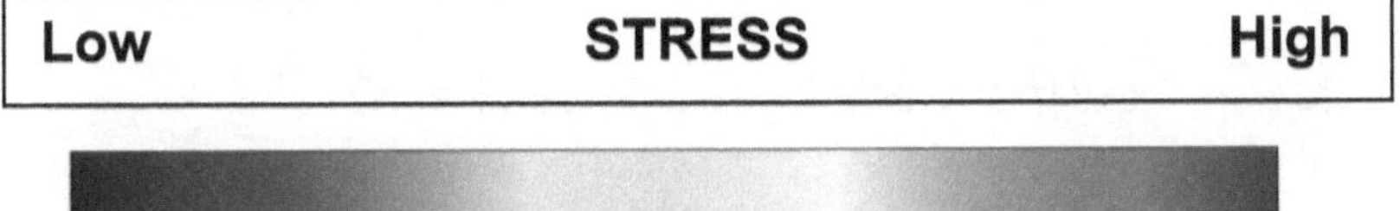

WARNING!

- A Bitch's initial statements are often hostile, producing resentment and withdrawal of others.

- A Son-of-a-Bitch's tone is often accusatory and blaming, placing others on the defensive.
- Bitches and Sons-of-Bitches often fail to explain their requirements or wishes clearly, and then react with anger at others for not performing tasks

adequately.

- They often chronically vacillate on their needs, quibbling about insignificant issues.
- They try to overwhelm others with needless demands and details.

Our research shows a larger proportion of S.O.B.s in areas of authority. These people, although not necessarily breaking the law or policy of an organization, often stretch the rules, manipulate policy, and misuse the law for their own selfish gain. The S.O.B. often knows the law or rules better than most and deviously takes advantage of those who do not.

Rate Your Company/Organization

1. How many employees do you have?

2. How many Bitches or S.O.B.s do you work with?

3. Status of the Bitches or S.O.B.s at work:

   Executive #_____   Supervisor #_____

   Manager #_____   Employees #_____

4.   Amount of stress the Bitch or S.O.B. causes:

#1 Bitch/S.O.B.   Lots   Some   Little

#2 Bitch/S.O.B.   Lots   Some   Little

#3 Bitch/S.O.B.   Lots   Some   Little

5.   Does the Bitch or S.O.B. know s/he is a Bitch or S.O.B.?

Bitch 1 _____

Bitch 2 _____

Bitch 3 _____

6.   Does the Bitch or S.O.B. know others view them as such?

Bitch 1 _____

Bitch 2 _____

Bitch 3 _____

7.   Do they care?

Bitch 1 _____
Bitch 2 _____

Bitch 3 _____

Workplace Bitch or S.O.B. Evaluation

Question	Always	Often	Sometimes	Never
Is the person rude to others?	4	3	2	1
Is the person discourteous to others?	4	3	2	1
Is the person condescending to others?	4	3	2	1
Is the person overbearing?	4	3	2	1
Does the person act as if they are smarter than most people?	4	3	2	1
Does the person act as if they are better than other people?	4	3	2	1
Does the person constantly criticize others?	4	3	2	1
Does the person suck up to the boss?	4	3	2	1
Does the person put others down?	4	3	2	1
Is the person arrogant?	4	3	2	1

Question	Always	Often	Some-times	Never
Does the person disrespect others?	4	3	2	1
Does the person smoke or drink too much?	4	3	2	1
Does the person devalue the work and contributions of others?	4	3	2	1
Does the person abuse other employee/ coworkers?	4	3	2	1
Does the person ignore those who they feel cannot help them?	4	3	2	1
Does the person have difficulty working with others?	4	3	2	1
Does the person resent the achievements of others?	4	3	2	1
Is the person committed to themselves over the company and its employees?	4	3	2	1

| Does the person misrepresent their accomplishments? | 4 | 3 | 2 | 1 |

Question	Always	Often	Some-times	Never
Is the person always complaining?	4	3	2	1
Does the person dominate others?	4	3	2	1
Do they withhold important information?	4	3	2	1
Does he/she blame others for their mistakes?	4	3	2	1
Does the person take advantage of weaker employees?	4	3	2	1
Does the person avoid working with others?	4	3	2	1
Does the person take credit for others' achievements or ideas?	4	3	2	1
TOTAL	_____	_____	_____	_____

Score 4 points for each "Always" answer.

Score 3 points for each "Often" answer.

Score 2 point for each "Sometimes" answer.

Score 1points for each "Never" answer.

Jobs with greater numbers of Bitches and Sons-of-Bitches include:

Rating	Career
#1	Lawyers
#2	Media
#3	Politicians
#4	Government
#5	Socialist
#6	Collections
#7	Executives/Managers

Some may say the above positions have more stress than other jobs; however, this is not the case. Senior employees with more knowledge about their situations tend to have less stress than other employees. For example, Air Traffic Controllers have a lot of on the job stress but a normal S.O.B. rating.

People with the nicest job ratings (lowest Bitch ratings) include:

1. Priests & Nuns
2. Ministers & Rabbis
3. Hostesses
4. Janitors
5. Sales
6. Marketing
7. Nurses
8. Doctors
9. Receptionists
10. Therapists
11. Waitpersons
12. Teachers
13. Human Resources
14. Customer Service
15. Judges

Effective Bitch or S.O.B. Stress Training

First-

Isolating the S.O.B.'s or Bitch's impact by identifying the organizational costs including absenteeism, workplace injuries, worker compensation claims, medical cost, and measuring employee stress levels resulting in lost productivity.

Second-

Implementation of a thorough stress management education and training program which includes an understanding of psychological, medical, and personal aspects of stress and the impact Bitches and Sons-of-a-Bitches have on fellow employees.

Third-

Teaching the benefits of applying Bitch stress management treatments and coping skills to all employees. Skills such as relaxation techniques, biofeedback, communication, exercise, and diet improvements have been shown to help.

Written Warnings

When all else fails in getting the point across to a Bitch at work - try a warning notice (see Conclusion). Even verbal discussions and written warnings sometimes fail to change a person with a sever S.O.B. affliction.

If this happens, see to it the S.O.B. gets a copy of this book and a personalized certificate like the sample at the book's end. A word of caution, if you decide to give a person the Bitch or S.O.B. certificate and this book, you do so at your own risk. There may be some dire consequences. Some people take it better than others. Before presenting them with this "gift" be certain they have earned it.

Chapter Five
Socializing with a Bitch
or a Son-of-a-Bitch

Socializing with a Bitch or a Son-of-a-Bitch is a real challenge, because one never knows when they will embarrass, humiliate, disgust, or anger you. They know just how to zero in on what they perceive as your faults, fallacies, failings, and secrets, and use them at the most inappropriate times. The best piece of advice here is to get out of their line of sight and thus, the line of fire.

If you are the sort who stands up to this type of person, prepare for battle - wearing your bullet proof vest, helmet, and boots.

Combat is their forte. They love to see people redden with anger or embarrassment because of what they have said or done. Some S.O.B.s are full of apologies after the damage is done. However, one must remember this is how they entertain themselves and get the power fix (albeit false) they need. Often the Bitch or S.O.B. thinks they are among the chosen few who do not have to abide by the rules of etiquette or the laws of the land. They think they make the rules.

A gathering of any sort is fertile ground for an S.O.B.'s enormous ego. It is the perfect venue for their exaggerated stories about themselves and the ideal setting for them to show off their supposed mental agility by picking on whoever happens to be in their way. They are quite cunning because they know enough to pick on someone they are sure won't fight back or is at a temporary disadvantage.

At social gatherings, Bitches are not comfortable when they are not in control. If only they would learn to control themselves.

THE TALKATIVE BITCH

We have all been trapped by the Bitch who won't shut up long enough to let anyone get a word in, no matter what. Have you ever had to deal with one of these Bitches? They go on and on while you wait patiently for her to turn blue from lack of oxygen, but it never happens. This incessant babbling causes much frustration and irritation among others.

Among bitches, there is also the incessant complainer who absolutely cannot find anything good in her life. The S.O.B. doesn't have enough sense to appreciate all the good in his life. Both are psychic energy vampires and their own worst enemies. They drain the compassion from others to the point they are avoided.

THE S.O.B. AS A LATECOMER

This section pertains to the S.O.B. who is habitually late. The individual who is late for dinner one time because of an honest delay is forgiven; while the habitually late person is a Son-of-a-Bitch. They act as though they are doing you a favor by showing up at all. Have you ever noticed how these S.O.B.s never invite people to their place? What exactly are they afraid of? We have all tried to give them, at least, a one hour head start on everyone else, right? How is it, then, they still end up late? They are very inconsiderate to others.

THE PHONEY

Often a Bitch wears a "nice" mask to social events and fakes everyone out. She will seem very nice to strangers but proceed to slice up and tear apart someone before long. Please beware, even in her nice mood, she can and will insult and incite.

S.O.B.s go through great pains to appear smart and clever, enjoying every minute of their attack. And then wonder why he doesn't have any friends. This is the pure work of a tyrannical Bitch and a despotic Son-of-a-Bitch. If they do have friends, those friends are super wimps or look and act just like the Bitch or S.O.B. because it is the only way the relationship can work. They are always looking for ways to be critical of someone or something.

THE SNOB

God forbid the Bitch excels at anything or has any children. And worst yet, should the Bitch or S.O.B. have children who excel at anything because now they become even more insufferable - blatant braggarts who never divulge the real facts about their kids. Perhaps, this is because they never see their kids for the problems they are. They are often a wet blanket at any social event they attend. The bottom-line is they are socially inept because they are immensely socially insecure.

The Report Card for the Bitch or S.O.B.

The following is a Report Card you can create for the person or persons you encounter as Bitches and S.O.B.s. If you are so inclined you may even send it to them or ask us to send it anonymously if you like. This is just a sampling of the different types of Bitches and S.O.B.s you may have to deal with. You may, of course, add to the list.

The Report Card for the Bitch or the S.O.B.

Key:

A = Almost a Bitch or S.O.B.

B = A Bitch or S.O.B.

C = A Controlling Bitch or S.O.B.

D = A very Difficult Bitch or S.O.B.

E = An Extreme Bitch or S.O.B.

F = A Total Failure

Name:______________________________________

Type	A	B	C	D	E	F
The Bitch or S.O.B. to the Hostess						
The Talkative S.O.B. or Bitch						
The Party Bitch or S.O.B.						
The Incessant Complainer						
The Latecomer						
The Phony S.O.B. or Bitch						
The Snob						
The Clerk is a Jerk						
The S.O.B. or Bitch Waiter						
The Bureaucratic S.O.B or Bitch						
The Town's Official Bitch or S.O.B						
Type	A	B	C	D	E	F

The Waiting Room							
The Road Warrior							
Actors							
Lawyers							
Media							
Politicians							
Administrators							
Teachers							
Others							

Additional Comments:_______________________________

____

____

THE NIGHT CLUB SCENE

For young people most nightclubs are fun and entertaining places to go. In addition, the majority of people who go to nightclubs are good people out to have a fun time enjoying good entertainment and dancing.

We probably can agree nightclubs come in all degrees of good and bad. S.O.B.'s and Bitches' destructive and dishonest ways can thrive in places like nightclubs. The drunken or dishonest S.O.B. or Bitch now has an excuse to be obnoxious, unfaithful, or worst. People can sometimes let down their defenses and become too trusting. Some people are lonely, desperate, and needing attention or affection. With fights, sexual assaults, abductions, and theft, this is sometimes the place where you can completely lose faith in the fact there are good, honest, and faithful people in the world.

The Suggested Solution: Avoidance and guarded behavior is advised. These people can be dangerous.

THE SON-OF-BITCHES OF THE ROADWAYS

This S.O.B. is a treacherous egomaniac. He weaves in and out of traffic leaving others to pick up the pieces of the accidents he has no idea he caused. S.O.B.s try to push vehicles out of their way with flashing lights, blasting horns, and tailgating. Why don't we ever see them get pulled over by the police?

The Suggested Solution: Do not let your ego get in the way, instead get out of the way as soon as possible, let the S.O.B. go, and dial 911 to report them.

Others are insane predators. These S.O.B.s chase or follow you for some perceived encounter.

The Suggested Solution: Pray for Divine Intervention. If you don't pray, good luck.

Then there is the S.O.B. who must have received his license from hell because he doesn't seem to know any of the rules of the road.

For example: He runs red lights. When there is an obstruction on his side of the road, he will not stop for oncoming traffic but will continue into the lane of oncoming traffic totally expecting you to do whatever it takes to let him go. This is misplaced positive thinking on his part.

The Suggested Solution: Don't get defensive. As with any wild animal, never make eye contact because if you do you are in for a terrible experience. Never, never, never give the finger. This is like adding gasoline to a fire. There are times when some driving S.O.B. predators have guns and are crazy enough to use them, and you never know whether they do or not.

Don't chance antagonizing these S.O.B.s, it's not worth getting killed over. Remember you have a family who loves you and wants you around for a while longer.

Slow drivers can be real Bitches, too. We all know they can be just as dangerous as the speeders and weavers, if not worse because they will cause good drivers to take chances passing when they would prefer not to do so. All rule books should instruct slow drivers to pull over and let the cars behind them pass.

SOME CLERKS ARE JERKS

First and foremost, if you are a good clerk, this will not apply to you in any way. Some clerks reinforce the old saying, "Clerks are Jerks." There are the clerks who are too busy talking to their co-workers OR ON THEIR PHONES OR COMPUTERS to help you. Other clerks are as slow as molasses. They obviously hate their jobs. There are those clerks who have a bad attitude and are sarcastic and those clerks who can't or won't find a solution to your particular problem, and can't be bothered to point you in the right direction.

The Suggested Solutions: If the management is unaware help them out and inform them of the S.O.B.'s behavior. If the management is as bad as the clerk, boycott the store.

THE BITCHY CUSTOMER

Yes, we have poor clerks with limited training. We also have some sales agents who do not like their job or customers. Then, we have the Bitch who is the customer from hell. They yell at the clerk for a store policy issue which she can't solve. The Bitch or S.O.B doesn't have the decency to be polite.

THE S.O.B. IN THE RESTAURANT/HOTEL

The restaurant scene is fertile ground for a Son-of-a-Bitch. This is among his favorite stomping grounds both as a customer and as waiter. The S.O.B. of a customer is often with someone else who ends up embarrassed while he abuses the waitresses.

The Bitch finds fault with everything in sight. Besides being impatient with waiting, she huffs and puffs and tries to blow the place up with her caustic remarks.

THE BITCH WITH THE CHILDREN FROM HELL

It is a Bitch who allows her children to run around, yell, or wail in public places.

The Suggested Solution: Yell and run in the opposite direction.

GOVERNMENTAL BUREAUCRACIES

Talk about people who serve the public with bad attitudes. Governmental Bureaucracies are a real Bitch. Have you ever been caught in one of those merry-go-rounds? It is, indeed, a circus with one exception; no one is enjoying themselves even though there are a lot of clowns around. They do manage to get you to jump through all kinds of hoops. These S.O.B.s go in one of two different ways. They either yes, yes, yes you or no, no, no you to death with absolutely no intention of being of service to the public they are supposed to be serving. Have you ever wondered what they're doing all day? The worse part of this situation is we are paying them to be in office and to be miserable to us. Funny thing is they used to be nice people. Now some are bitchy, complacent and unhelpful. The more they deny or ignore everyone's needs or requests for help, the more grandiose sense of power they get.

Small town employees are so much nicer and helpful. Big government officials are more often than not a great example of abusing the power with which they were entrusted.

The best advice to these S.O.B.s is: BE FAIR, BE FLEXIBLE, AND BE COOPERATIVE. Remember who has the last say. Stop your nit-picking, overly critical, demanding, nasty, vengeful, passive aggressive nonsense. Stop being self-serving by blocking actions fair to others because it gives you this super sense of power and hate to see someone else get ahead. The public has hired you to do a job for them, not to become some bureaucratic god in the sky who will give you bureaucratic brownie points for being a super-duper Bitch. Relax, be the public's friend - not the enemy. Only fair and just people should be allowed to apply for the jobs.

And then, there are the Newbies who are trying to take over, think they know how to run the government better, and want to change everything. However, there are some Newbies who don't want to change a thing and block every little advancement.

MEDICAL PROFESSIONALS AND OTHERS WITH WAITING ROOMS

Most medical doctors and other professionals are nice people, but a few are S.O.B.s too. These few could care less how long you wait in their waiting room, suffering from some illness, ailment, or injury. They are actually inflicting pain rather than curing it. Maybe that's the purpose. Have you ever heard a doctor apologize for keeping you waiting? Even if they did, they really don't care that you have a life outside the waiting room. Everyone who has ever visited a doctor's office has fallen victim to this waiting room torture. Have you ever bumped into a doctor waiting in a waiting room? We are often subjected to outrageous assumptions about how we live our lives so they can grind us in and grind us out and make as many bucks as possible in one day.

It seems the only thing they learn is how to sock it to us. Every decision made about you is all about their wallet. They won't order tests because every test subtracts from their profits.

The Suggested Solution:

1. Do not wait any longer than what you deem reasonable and fair to you.

2. Send the doctor a report card.

RATE THE SOCIAL BITCH or S.O.B.

	Always	Often	Some	Never
Boisterous	4	3	**2**	1
Vulgar	4	3	2	1
Impolite	4	3	2	1
Sarcastic	4	3	**2**	1
Make fun of People	4	3	2	1
Insulting	4	3	2	1
Controlling	4	3	2	1
Self-Centered	4	3	2	1
Self-Righteous	4	3	2	1
Obnoxious	4	3	2	1
Loud/Yell	4	3	2	1
Braggart	4	3	2	1

	Always	Often	Some	Never
Bad Manners	4	3	2	1
Redundant	4	3	2	1
Overeat, drink	4	3	2	1
Untruthful	4	3	2	1
Unfair to Others	4	3	2	1
Inconsiderate	4	3	2	1
False Compassion	4	3	2	1
Poor Communicator	4	3	2	1
Smoke in Crowds	4	3	2	0
Mean	4	3	2	0
Abrupt	4	3	2	0
Inconsiderate	4	3	2	0
Spit in Public	4	3	2	0
Gossip	4	3	2	0
Swear Too Much	4	3	2	0
Complain Incessantly	4	3	2	0
TOTALS				

Score 4 points for each "Always" answer.

Score 4 points for each "Almost Always" answer.

Score 3 points for each "Often" answer.

Score 2 points for each "Sometimes" answer.

Refer to page 86 for the definition of each score and category.

To Be or Not to Be a Famous Bitch or S.O.B. Survey

Below is a key to identifying the degree to which someone is a Bitch or S.O.B. as determined by a national poll conducted and these famous people. They are judged on the traits listed below.

Key:

- A Super Bitch or S.O.B. is a person with very few redeeming traits 100 percent of the time. They alienate everyone with whom they come in contact.
- A Bitch or S.O.B. is a very mean person 75 percent or more of the time.
- A Bitchy person is a very difficult person at least 50 percent or more of the time.
- A Moody or Difficult person is a good person but unpredictable, at least 25 percent of the time.
- Nice means someone is a good person approximately 100 percent of the time. They have a good character, good values, good morals, a good sense of humor, and a good attitude.

All celebrities and notables are judged on their public images as reported by any source available, and according to the majority of the common ordinary citizen's perception. Only a short list of traits was used to qualify a Nice Person. You will be surprised how many celebrities cannot make the rating of Nice Person.

Do any famous people qualify as a Bitch in your opinion? Rate each one you select according to your opinion of their public image and see if it matches up with other opinions.

This is not to say someone who has a bad hair day (other than Cruella de Vil) every once in a while, is a S.O.B. And there are those types who run a tight ship and are not Bitches. These people are often demanding but are found to be fair and just. And it is not to say people who are opinionated are Bitches. They can still be fair, just, and moral. We are talking about bad intentioned people - those with a selfish or biased agenda who scored low in our survey. Television news people who give the perception of bias in dealing with others lost some ground; as did individuals with a very conservative or very liberal bias lost points even if they scored high in other areas.

The following key was used to interpret the results of the nationwide poll:

Angel = 0-10

Someone Special = 11-25

Nice = 26-35

Normal = 36-49

Difficult = 50-60

Bitchy/Bad = 61-70

Bitch or S.O.B. = 71-89

Super Bitch or S.O.B. = 90-112

Angel - Saint: 0-10 Points

This is a wonderful person. Keep this person in your life. If they want something, get it or do it for them. Protect your relationship at all costs. IMPORTANT: Do not show this person your rating if it is over 30.

Special: 11-25 Points

This is a good person. You should feel proud to be related to or associated with them. Do what you can to develop an even stronger relationship.

Nice: 26-35 Points

This person goes out of their way to do good deeds but sometimes make mistakes.

Normal: 36-49 Points

This is a good person with human flaws which should be tolerated or overlooked from time to time. Stick with them.

Difficult/Moody: 50-60 Points

This person can get upset or mad a bit too often. You should be careful to be sure they do not have a negative effect on your family. Try to talk things over more often. These people can be biased, untrustworthy, and sometimes self-serving.

Bitchy/Bad: 61-70 Points

This person is living on the edge. Protect yourself from undue stress and heartache by seriously evaluating your relationship to him or her to prevent disaster. Protect any children from exposure to this person's negative behavior. They can be sneaky and deceiving, vindictive, and unreasonable.

Bitch or S.O.B.: 71-89 Points

This person is a Bitch. You had better get a plan for self-defense before it's too late. You have only one life; why live it with a S.O.B.?

Super Bitch or S.O.B.: 90-112 Points

This person is a reign of terror; miserable plus miserable. Seek "E.B.T."(Emergency Bitch Treatment) and consider moving as soon as possible.

Survey Sample

Name of Possible Bitch or S.O.B.	Public Rating	Your Rating	Comments
Media			

Political Notables

Barack Obama President of the United States			Promises kept Results Family Personal Spiritual Patriotism Constitution Past behavior Honesty
Donald Trump President of the United States			Promises kept Results Family Personal Spiritual Patriotism Constitution Past Behavior Honesty
You Select a Person			

Sports Figures

Name of Possible Bitch or S.O.B.	Public Rating	Your Rating	Comments
Tom Brady			

Name of Possible Bitch or S.O.B.	Public Rating	Your Rating	Comments
Oprah Winfrey			

Name of Possible Bitch or S.O.B.	Public Rating	Your Rating	Comments
George Washington			

TV/Movie Figures

Name of Possible Bitch or S.O.B.	Public Rating	Your Rating	Comments
Brad Pitt			

Business Figures

Name of Possible Bitch or S.O.B.	Public Rating	Your Rating	Comments
Bill Gates			

Family

Name of Possible Bitch or S.O.B. Mother	Public Rating	Your Rating	Comments

Name of Possible Bitch or S.O.B.	Public Rating	Your Rating	Comments

Co-Workers

Name of Possible Bitch or S.O.B.	Public Rating	Your Rating	Comments

Chapter Six
The Psychology and Development of a Bitch and a Son-of-A-Bitch

By now, you certainly want to know where Bitches and S.O.B.s come from. Well, there are two main ways Bitches and Sons-of-a-Bitch appear:

1.   Heredity

2.   Environment

Heredity means one is predisposed to receive the "B" (Bitch) Gene. The B-Gene is still a greatly misunderstood concept. Much research is yet to be done. Just like the First-Born Theory, in which people believe the first child born in a family is most likely to succeed, people believe 10 percent of the population is genetically predisposed to developing a Son-of-a-Bitch personality from the B-Gene.

This theory has two components:

1. Her mother was a Bitch, and her mother before her.

2. He is a Son-of-a-Bitch, as his father before him.

If your mother is a Bitch or your father is a Son-of-a-Bitch, then you would be well served to be certain your B-Genes do not dominate your life. If you wish, you may try to control your B-Genes. It may take some work, but you can do it.

The emergence of the Bitch Gene first appeared in the 20th century. It is commonly found in people whose excessive focuses are social class, money, power, status, and greed. All these factors also play a role in Bitch or S.O.B. development.

The most commonly accepted theory is Bitch Development is 10 percent genetic and 90 percent environmentally learned behavior. This belief has continued throughout the 21st century. Intelligence or cognitive stratification is a much smaller factor than most Bitches would have you believe. Our research shows no measurable difference in IQ from Bitches and Sons-of-Bitches to the rest of the population. The Bitch only thinks she is smarter than the rest of us, therefore, more entitled to preferential treatment.

There are not more Bitches among smart women.

Most researchers believe Bitch Behavior has been learned. We also found the S.O. B. has the knowledge and ability to change his behavior but chooses not to for selfish reasons.

Statistics and Impact

How many Bitches and S.O.B.s are there? Estimates are 15 Million in the U.S. No one knows exactly but we do know one thing - *there are way too many.*

BEWARE! BITCHES AND S.O.B.S DON'T HAVE STRESS, THEY GIVE IT! If you know anyone who has said this or thinks like this, you are up against a monster.

Four hundred billion dollars are spent on stress every year. Our best guess is Bitches and S.O.B.s create 30 percent of this total.

We know a large percentage of all diseases and disorders are directly or indirectly attributable to stress. The Bitch and S.O.B. have made a great contribution to this problem.

Five hundred thousand people die every year from heart attacks - the biggest killer of both men and women. Guess who put most of them in the ground? The funny thing is hostility and over exertion is the number one cause of heart attacks. They just forgot to tell us it could be someone else's hostility that does us in. This must be the case because a lot of Bitches and S.O.B.s are out there on the loose.

Check out the charts below.

How Many Bitches and S.O.B.s Are There in Your Life?

_____Boss	_____Wife
_____Co-Workers	_____Husband
_____Mother	_____Partner
_____Father	_____Town/City Official(s)
_____Sister(s)	_____Neighbor(s)
_____Brother(s)	_____Friend(s)

If you have more than one, get immediate help to deal with this serious situation. Your health and welfare are in jeopardy.

Total Bitches and S.O.B.s in Your Life

	Bitches (women)	S.O.B.s (men)	Total
AT HOME	2.5M	0.5M	3.0M
AT WORK	1.0M	7.0M	8.0M
Super Bitch	1.5M	0.5M	2.0M
Bitch	2.5M	4.0M	6.5M
Sub Total	4.0M	4.5M	8.5M
Bitchy	16.0M	5.0M	21.0M
Difficult	15.0M	18.0M	33.0M
Total	**38.5M**	**35.0M**	**73.5M**

Possible S.O.B. or Bitch Profile

Male/Female

1. Married, single, or divorced

2. Currently in a bad mood

3. Between the ages of 18 and 100

4. Self-centered

5. Overweight and mean or lean and mean

6. Angry at the world

7. Loner

8. Scowl on their face

9. Rigid body posture

The S.O.B. tends to have had major family fights with parents or siblings while growing up. Although some are successful, they tend to be frustrated under-achievers, struggling to reach unrealistic unearned goals in their work and personal lives. Sometimes they feel they should be more recognized, and they become liars regarding past achievements not only to themselves but to others as well. Maintaining this lie can turn them into Bitches or S.O.B.s. Even exceptionally talented people with much success in one part of their lives may still feel unsatisfied.

This dissatisfaction can result in an attitude of entitlement without working for results at work, at home, or in relationships.

For example, "Rich Bitch" or rich SOB is a term difficult to understand. It shows that money may not make you happy.

A bright man, for example, who has failed in his chosen career may feel the government owes him a living without any achievement and resents all who have achieved success in their own personal life decisions. Sometimes they may even give up trying to achieve and insist the government pay their way through life, lashing out at people and policies which resist that selfish outlook.

Another extreme are the Sons-of-a-Bitches who may be talented in sports or entertainment, yet still believe they should get more recognition or better

sponsorship offers. When they do not, they behave
badly and become "Nasty Sons-of-a-Bitches."

Development

Let us take look at how the Bitch and the Son-of-a-
Bitch develop in five main areas. Normal people have
these decency skills in place.

These areas include:

1.   Perception - What life is all about

2.   Motivation - Why they act that way

3.   Learning - Life skills

4.   Personality - Interaction skills

5.   Social Behavior - Respect for
       others

Perception - They have a twisted perception of the
world, believing they are the center of the universe
and they should make decisions for those with whom
they associate.

Motivation - They are selfishly motivated. Give Me - Show Me -Take Me is their attitude. Their bases of behavior are solely built on what is in it for them.

Learning - They often have an exceptional area where they excel: singing, sports, business, communication. Other areas are often sub-par and they hide their inadequacies by focusing solely on their selected skill area.

Personality - Dominance, overbearing, and excessive criticism are the trademarks of the Bitch or S.O.B. They are often ungrateful for what they have and cynical toward the achievements of others.

Social Behavior - These people are anti-social loners. They socialize when it suits them and only when there is something to gain. They can sometimes associate well with other Bitchy People.

Being a Bitch or S.O.B. is a progressive disorder which can be controlled. As nice people, we might not believe the Bitch or S.O.B. is so bad. We may believe they will change. Forget it. They need help to arrest their Bitch Behavior. If they do not get help or want to change, you are in for a rougher time than you ever imagined.

Control, control, control. Bitches and S.O.B.s are control freaks. They are excellent at controlling their complete environment - the workplace, the home, and the social situations.

Some are bred this way. They genuinely think they are the only ones who count because they are better, went to all the best schools, best this, and best that, so they deduce they are the best - better than anyone else. The result – they believe whatever anyone has to say or do cannot be as interesting, so why give them the time of day. They are afraid to be real and down to earth.

Another type is the Bitch who has a not so illustrious background and is forever trying to hide it because they might be thought of poorly by his family and/or neighbors or ethnic group. They are trying to pretend they are blue-blooded. They use this snobby demeanor to ward off people in general. They really are anti-social and suffer from low self-esteem. They do not understand that secure people are very comfortable with everyone including themselves.

Can these Bitches change? Well, yes, but, they must want to change. Sometimes they may have a fantastic conversion. This is good but they still may not respect other perspectives on the world. A morally superior attitude could become a very Bitchy attitude.

Again, it needs to be mentioned, if these people are accepting and secure, they will accept all people as long as they are civil and have moral values.

Lots of those of the first type will go through life genuinely thinking they are very good people, doing good deeds, donating time and money to charities, while never really "getting it."

What is meant by getting it? They never realize what insecure beings they really are. Their ingrained behavior is a suit of armor against being real. They don't know how to be genuine because they had no positive role models and simply were never taught. An example would be the difference between a genuine woman like Mother Theresa and a cartoonish character like Cruella de Vil.

There is also the S.O.B. who would rather intimidate - hit first and never ask questions. Why? He may have been abused emotionally somewhere along the line. Unfortunately, in many instances, the emotionally abused becomes the abuser. They not only may have had a poor role model but also are so angry at the world they take it out on everyone. Don't turn your back on these types. Being abused is no excuse for becoming an abuser. No one, absolutely no one, has the right to hurt the innocent regardless of their excuse.

Their motto is: "Don't tread on me. I do the treading!"

The Bitch and her many Sons are not categories yet in the DSM IV or DSM IVR (Diagnostic and Statistical Manual of Mental Disorders), though they ought to be. It is strange that the Bitch makes sure everyone else ends up with one of the listed disorders. We must take responsibility for ourselves and make sure we stay healthy and wise, or we will end up as one of the diseases or disorders in the DSM IV.

- Can you look around and see the debris left in the wake of a Bitch's outburst?
- Are there ghost-like echoes in the halls of your organization from past victims of the Bitch or S.O.B.?
- Have there been fierce Bitch Battles which have left valiant warrior bodies to wither away in time?
- Has your organization or home surrendered to the ruthless activities of the Bitch and become a victim of her conquest?

Here is how to win back your freedom, your integrity, and your self-esteem without surrendering to the dark forces of the Bitch or Son-of-a-Bitch.

Remember, this is a battle of wills. You can break through to victory over the stress the Bitch inflicts. You do not have to break down and submit to her invalid demands. You must be strong of will to turn her dark power to your advantage.

You accomplish this by using your inner strength. You must find an alternative to absorbing the stress which the Bitch intends to inflict. Even if there is no physical escape from the work or home environment in which the Bitch or S.O.B. stalks their prey, you can survive with pride.

Chapter Seven
Treatment

What treatments are available for a Bitch or S.O.B.? This is an important question; however, more critical is what you should do if you are under a Bitch attack or caught in an environment controlled by a Son-of-a-Bitch.

We have been there, too. We know what you are going through. Remember, it is not your problem - the Bitch or S.O.B. has the problem. They struggle to get control of everything, which is an impossible task.

Their behavior is often compulsive. You are powerless to stop them. They often are in denial, believing they are right and everyone else is wrong. They excuse their personal behavior by projecting blame on others. You must not accept the blame and thereby damage your own self-esteem.

Recommendation: Stop being a victim. Only when we stop fighting the Bitch or hoping, no, praying the S.O.B. will change, can we retain control of our lives. Tell the Bitch or S.O.B. you will not argue with them. Detach yourself from their behavior. They are the problem, not you.

It does not take a shrink to see that a person is a Bitch or S.O.B. Just evaluate what is happening calmly and rationally and you will realize their behavior is not your responsibility.

If the person in your life is Bitching more each day and things are getting progressively worse, then listen closely:

1. Do not treat the S.O.B. like a child.

2. Do not check up on them.

3. Do not nag or Bitch back.

4. Do not scold or get into a fight.

5. Do not threaten.

Why not? Well, because things will get worse for the Bitch. Your neutral-distant behavior will create confusion in the Son-of-a-Bitch's plan of shared misery. They will begin to learn you are not taking it anymore. The Son-of-a-Bitch must realize the situation is so serious they could lose you.

You can help them only when the Bitch or S.O.B. knows their behavior is fruitless and you will no longer be controlled by them. Remember, this realization cannot be forced - the Bitch must see it on their own.

The road ahead is not smooth, but you can get there. The Son-of-a-Bitch must follow the steps in the road to recovery starting on page 124. Your job is to stay strong and remember the Bitch or S.O.B. was not born this way; it took time to develop and it will take time for them to get better.

Learning to tolerate feelings associated with the Bitch
or S.O.B. is a major task for most victims. Do not do
anything rash or violent. You may become
desperately angry or helpless. Remember, the Son-
of-a-Bitch wants to control you and you cannot let
them. Don't fight with them. Learn the power of
silence.

Essential Steps to Recovery for the Bitch or One of her Many Sons

Now you have confirmed what you suspected all
along. You are living with or working for a Bitch or
Son-of-a-Bitch. What can you do about it? Well, you
have some choices:

- Do nothing and continue getting verbally abused.

- Try to survive and improve your situation.

- Confront the Bitch.

- Send the Bitch an assessment and wait for
improvement.

- If married, go to Reno for a quick divorce.

- If employed by one, update your resume.

- Your best bet is to send them a copy of this book as
you follow the recommendations on the following
pages.

• Send them a Warning Letter.

Remember: The Bitch and S.O.B. are more enthralled with the workplace than any other venue, tending to believe the workplace gives them a license to be a Bitch or S.O.B.

Follow these Psychological Steps:

1. ***Remember you are in this, both alone and together.*** There may be others who suffer, but you must be accountable for your own actions. God helps those who help themselves. You will not be able to help others unless you can help yourself first. Look out for #1 first.

2. ***The customer is #3.*** It is simple - the person who said the customer is #1 is wrong. Take care of yourself and you will be better able to take care of #2, the family or organization. If you and your family or organization are okay, then you will be able to take care of #3, the customer or friends. Whether you have internal or external customers, you can make them feel like #1 only when they are really #3. By the way, the Bitch is last.

3. ***Reduce the Bitch's emotional impact.*** If the Bitch or S.O.B. is the cause of the excessive

emotional strain and pressure, find ways to isolate the impact their Bitchy actions have on you. Do not count on upper management, a revolution, a layoff, or anything other than yourself. Do not view protecting your feelings as a burden - it is a responsibility only you can fill.

4. ***A.C.T.*** Accept the situation, environment, Bitch or S.O.B. with whom you are dealing. Challenge yourself to stay under control and be as cool, calm, and collected as possible. Act to improve your situation. Do not try to change the Bitch or S.O.B., instead get your job or responsibilities completed to the best of your ability. Stay flexible and do not take on excess emotional baggage. Adjust to changes in a professional way. This does not mean you have to agree with the Bitch, but don't let disagreements bruise your spirit or drain your energy, which is key to helping you and your organization prosper.

5. ***Don't act like a victim.*** Hold your head up and your pride within. Let your frustration about bad decisions go. Move on. Do not dwell in past events you cannot change. Self-pity is not attractive and threatens your future. Remain productive. You are accountable for how you feel.

6. ***Embrace Change/Control Stress.*** Change

happens, especially at work, whether we want it or not. This goes for the Bitch or S.O.B., too. The Bitch will not last as long as you embrace change. Keep your attitude positive about change. Pretty soon, the Bitch or S.O.B. will have to change the way they deal with you. A positive, nice person is the Bitch's worst fear because of their lack of class and because they are transparent around you. The change and stress are not going away. Make sure you control it within you.

7. ***<u>You cannot control the Bitch or S.O.B.</u>*** Though you can try to influence events which have a positive effect on you and your organization, it is difficult to accept that you cannot change the Bitch, especially if you care for them or even love them. Ask yourself if the struggle to change someone else makes sense. Save your psychological energy.

8. ***<u>Keep pace with events.</u>*** This does not mean keep pace with the S.O.B. Follow the direction set by the organization's or family's needs. Do not let the S.O.B. fool you into following them. They may be trying to deceive you to make you look bad. Be careful, because sometimes the Bitch lures you in with goals which seem to be consistent with the organization or the family only to catch you off guard later when you are in a trusting mood.

9. ***Do not be vulnerable.*** If the Bitch or S.O.B.
    picks on you, reduce their options - get rid of
    bad habits, do not procrastinate, be neater, do
    things right the first time, have a positive
    attitude, do not dwell on the past, and
    contribute more than your share. Eliminate
    their idea of you as an easy target by being
    more productive.

10. ***Think positive.*** Work on your self-control.
    Look forward to the future. Do not show your
    fear. Do not go home or to work drained,
    because it shows. Dispirited, weary people act
    like victims and they soon will be screaming
    and running away from their life and work,
    hiding from the Bitch. Do not let the Bitch be
    the anchor dragging behind you. Do not run or
    hide, but do not fight either. Fighting is too
    emotionally fatiguing and is just what the Bitch
    wants to get you to waste your energy on
    negative things. Stay positive. Let the Bitch
    wallow in misery without you.

11. ***Know when to stand your ground.*** Do not
    pick battles of principle whimsically. Choose
    issues to confront the S.O.B. which are factual
    and the ones you are most likely to win or
    come out ahead. Do not try to stop the Bitch's
    freight train or defend the indefensible issue.
    Use issues the organization or family will

support. Do not buck the odds. Carefully evaluate the consequences of your actions. Do not pick hopeless causes either – in which case you are letting the S.O.B. choose the battlefield and the weapons. Do not give major attention to minor problems; which makes you appear as if you are blowing things out of proportion for no good reason. Choose reversible decisions; if they are wrong, do not choose irreversible issues to debate.

12. ***Stay involved.*** Do not give up emotionally – it shows. Do not drive wedges between your boss/spouse and yourself even if they are a Bitch. Stay committed to positive behavior - it will pay off.

13. ***Carry a mirror and use it.*** Do not avoid compromise. Emphasize preventing problems in your actions. Evaluate yourself. How much do you contribute to the S.O.B.'s behavior? Do not antagonize or taunt them. Stay on track and do not shy away from solutions which can ease tension and emotional stress from the S.O.B. Be more tolerant. Choose actions of correction not confusion. Stay out of the Red Zone and remember - there is no comfort zone. This effort takes work and commitment to enhance your emotional well-being.

14. ***Time marches on.*** No Bitch lasts. They may have money and power for a while, but they

eventually find themselves living with sadness and loneliness with few, if any, friends. You may notice, a Bitch has real difficulty with any personal or intimate interaction. Time will catch us all. Let it catch you in control of your emotional and physical health.

15. ***Resistance is fruitful.*** Resist the temptation to behave like the S.O.B. Forget payback and focus on pay off. Evil behavior makes everyone feel bad and causes bad behavior. Set a good example by acting responsibly, and explaining why you are doing what you are doing. Let your good intentions be clear when you resist negative behavior. Let no one be a witness for the S.O.B. Create an environment where people know they will feel better when they resist negative behavior. Let the S.O.B. see the resistance, feel the resistance, and subsequently they will fear the resistance. Life is a marathon - make it a long one and do not let the S.O.B. take you out of the race. Be sure they know you are sticking around, and your resistance will be fruitful.

Victim Recommendations

1. Put yourself first once in a while.

2. Do not devalue your feelings or opinions.

3. Protect yourself from unfair treatment or criticism.

4. You have the right to responsibly express your feelings, thoughts, ideas, or opinions.

5. You have the right to say no.

6. You have the right to ignore Bitchy behavior.

7. You do not have to justify your existence or presence.

8. You have a right to recognition for your achievements.

9. You do not have to take the blame for others' mistakes or behavior.

10. You do not have to be a mind reader.

11. You do not have to take verbal abuse.

12. You can get sick from being pushed around.

13. Do not be a servant.

14. Take time for yourself.

15. Do not be threatened.

16. Do your fair share of the work, but not all the work all the time.

17. Do not yell – scream – demand - whine.

18. Be nice, no matter how hard it is.

19. Listen and clarify issues. Be firm, with erect
    body posture and direct eye contact.

20. Compromise, but do not always give in.

21. Set aside quiet time for yourself each day.

22. Plan your day's activities.

23. You do not have to be a perfectionist, but
    always do your best.

24. Cut off non-productive activities.

25. Do not call anyone a Bitch or one of her many
    sons.

26. Do not expect not to be yelled at or put down in
    some way.

27. Do not demand respect. They do not know
    what that means - the word is not in their
    vocabulary.

28. Evaluate the best options you have and act.
    Do not act rashly or out of anger.

29. Examine the past; continue what works. Stop
    doing what does not work.

30. Reward yourself occasionally.

Responding to the Bitch or S.O.B.

We have covered a lot of ground. You have learned what a Bitch or S.O.B. really is. You now know how they develop. You know how many there are, what behavior they exhibit, and why. We have even provided you with the best way to respond to them.

But what about those of you who want or feel you need more help? Well, we want to offer you every chance to change your life for the better. So, for those of you who want to take special and immediate action to respond to the Bitch or S.O.B. in your life, we have some options for you. With each of these options you should take precautions to protect your confidentiality. If you take these steps, do so with care. Do not do steps that may cause harm to anyone. Consider the following:

Conclusion

As I bring the book to a close, I'd like to state clearly that I have tried to avoid any psychological personality disorder diagnoses and simply stick with the fun, tongue-in-cheek dialogue. This information is not given in an effort to diagnose others but rather as an evaluation of how others treat us, as well as those we love, and care about.

While as the reader you may see similarities with terms you have heard like Narcissism or even Sociopath, but such correlations and evaluations should be left to professionals. Rather we should focus on the behavior directed at us, as well as those in our homes, workplaces, and social circles.

It is possible the Bitch or S.O.B. in your life has large clusters of the following behaviors toward you and so, you should take care to protect yourself and your loved ones.

Bitch and S.O.B. Cluster Behaviors to Watch Out For:

- Mean

- Insecure

- Superior attitude

- Entitled

- Takes advantage of others

- Wants to be the center of attention

- Lacks empathy

- Unreasonably demanding

- Overtly competitive

- Holds a grudge

- Unable to handle criticism

- Envious

- Filled with false charm

- Requires lots of praise

In the following pages, you will find some additional self-help tools you may want to use to aid you in protecting yourself and your family from the Bitches and S.O.B.s in your life. There is little to lose in taking action to protect yourself and so much to gain. Good Luck!

Additional Help

Book Only - Send a copy of this book anonymously to Bitches, S.O.B.s, or their victims.

Written Warning Letter - You can send the Bitch or S.O.B. a stern letter. This is for those of you who think this person truly deserves a written warning. You should also send the book.

Official Bitch or S.O.B. Registration - You could send the book plus an official classification letter to the person you formally rate a Bitch or S.O.B. This letter could inform them they are considered, by you, to be a Bitch or S.O.B. They could also receive a certificate of accomplishment and a reform contract they can sign if they choose to repent and forever give up their Bitchy ways.

Official Bitch/S.O.B. Warning

This is an Official Bitch or S.O.B. Warning! There have been complaints that your behavior is offensive to many with whom you live, work, or socialize. Frankly, the consensus is you have a despicable record of human interaction. Many feel there is still a chance for you to behave like a normal human being. For this reason, we hope you will read the enclosed book. You are encouraged to read the book in an effort to help you change. Your refusal to improve will result in more people who cannot stand your behavior. It may be difficult for you, but please try to be nice.

The Bitch or S.O.B. Letter

Dear Mr./Ms.(Name here)

It is our responsibility to inform you that you have been evaluated by those with whom you work, live, or socialize. This careful review of your behavior was conducted by those who know you best.

Because of your complete disregard for the feelings of those around you, you have received the title of "Bitch" or "Son-of-a- Bitch." It is irrelevant whether you agree or disagree with the findings of this report. You are officially classified as Bitch or S.O.B. This classification is due to your relentless and ruthless disregard and disrespect for the feelings of others. Your condescending attitude and repulsive behavior toward others has gone too far. It is time you were told how people feel about your behavior. You may view this letter with disdain, as you have viewed most other things, and discard it as of no consequence. On the other hand, you may view this opinion of you as a new awareness. If you do, there is hope for you. You can recover by:

1. Reading the enclosed book.

2. Carefully assessing your behavior.

3. Signing the Bitch/ S.O.B. Reform Contract.

4. Following the contract and changing your behavior.

We sincerely hope you try to get along with others in the future.

Sincerely,

Your Name

Bitch Reform Contract

1. I admit I am a Bitch or a Son-of-a-Bitch.

2. I now admit or realize my behavior has been selfish, mean, and hurtful to others.

3. I agree a portion of my life became unmanageable and I must turn away from the dark forces of my Bitch or S.O.B. behavior which controls me.

4. I promise to make a moral inventory of my behavior.

5. I confess my sinful behavior to my spouse, relative, friends, and employees.

6. I am now prepared to live life as a nicer person, no matter how hard it is for me.

7. *I humbly ask for forgiveness for those with whom I work and live.*

8. *I have made a list of all 100-500-1000-more people I have harmed.*

9. *I will try to make amends to these people I have harmed.*

10. *In the future, I will admit when I am wrong and not behave like a Bitch or S.O.B.*

11. *In the future, I will always try to be nice and resist my Bitch Behavior.*

____

Bitch or S.O.B. Signature
Date

ORDER FORM FOR ADDITIONAL HELP MATERIALS

Your Name:_______________________________________

Address:____

____

____

Phone: ____

FAX:____

Email:____

Number of Books Ordered: _____________________

Amount of Check Enclosed_______________________

Ship To:

Name: ____

Address:____

____

____

Phone:_______________

FAX:____

Email:____

Son of a Bitch Letter

Dear Mr. _____,

It is our responsibility to inform you have been evaluated by those with whom you work, live, and associate. This careful review of your behavior was an assessment over a long period and by many. Because of your unprofessionalism and your complete disregard for the feelings and hard work of others who you interact with, you have received the title of "<u>Son of a Bitch</u>." This is not a compliment or joke. You are a poor representative and an embarrassment. You look down upon the work of others. You resist the fine ideas of others because they are not yours and you make offensive, know-it-all comments driving others away.

It is irrelevant whether you agree or disagree with the findings of the report. The report was conducted by a number of others evaluating a wide range of personal and professional qualities. You are officially classified as a "Son of a Bitch." This classification is due to your continuous and bullying disregard and disrespect for the feelings of others. Your condescending attitude and repulsive behavior toward others has gone too far. It is time you were told how people feel about your behavior. Your nasty comments in meetings as well as your closed mind leaves others with a sour opinion about you, the organization, and things you purport to represent. You are chasing people away from you and a fine organization. You may view this letter with disdain as you have viewed most other things and disregard it as of no consequence. You may continue to not listen to the silent voices around you acting professionally and avoiding confrontation with you. On the other hand, you may view this opinion of yourself as a new awareness. If you do, there is hope for you.

You can recover if you: Admit your bad behavior; Admit you know much less than you pretend; Take a moral inventory; Apologize to others; Be nicer person towards family, friends, and all other professionals; Terminate nasty and negative jokes and comments.

(This letter is sent independently and anonymous, but authorized by at least 10 others.)

Bitch Letter

Dear Mrs./Ms. ____,

It is our responsibility to inform you that you have been evaluated by those with whom you work, live, and associate. This careful review of your behavior was an assessment over a long period and by many. Because of your unprofessionalism and your complete disregard for the feelings and hard work of others who you interact with, you have received the title of "_Bitch._" This is not a compliment or joke. You are a poor representative and an embarrassment. You look down upon the work of others. You resist the fine ideas of others because they are not yours and you make offensive, know-it-all comments driving others away.

It is irrelevant whether you agree or disagree with the findings of the report. The report was conducted by a number of others evaluating a wide range of personal and professional qualities. You are officially classified as a "Bitch." This classification is due to your continuous and bullying disregard and disrespect for the feelings of others. Your condescending attitude and repulsive behavior toward others has gone too far. It is time you were told how people feel about your behavior. Your nasty comments in meetings as well as your closed mind leaves others with a sour opinion about you, the organization, and things you purport to represent. You are chasing people away from you and a fine organization. You may view this letter with disdain as you *have viewed most other things and disregard it as of no consequence. You may continue to not listen to the silent voices around you acting professionally and avoiding confrontation with you. On the other hand, you may view this opinion of yourself as a new awareness. If you do, there is hope for you.*

You can recover if you: Admit your bad behavior; Admit you know much less than you pretend; Take a moral inventory; Apologize to others; Be nicer person towards family, friends, and all other professionals; Terminate nasty and negative jokes and comments.

(This letter is sent independently and anonymous, but authorized by at least 10 others.)